A Brief History of Golf

A Brief History of Golf

What Every Golfer Should
Know About the Game

by Alan Ross

WALNUT GROVE PRESS
Nashville, TN 37205

ISBN 1-887655-85-9

Material for this book was obtained mostly from secondary sources, primarily print media. While every effort was made to ensure the accuracy of these sources, the accuracy cannot be guaranteed. For additions, deletions, corrections or clarifications in future editions of this text, please write WALNUT GROVE PRESS.

Printed in the United States of America
1 2 3 4 5 6 7 8 9 10 • 98 99 00 01 02

ACKNOWLEDGMENTS
The author gratefully acknowledges the friendship, support, and wonderful opportunity extended by Dr. Criswell Freeman. Thanks also to the magnificent staff at Walnut Grove Press and to Karol Cooper for her inspiration and dedicated contributions both during and between rounds.

For Daren

Whose passion for golf continues unabated,
with the knowledge that the game is never fully learned

Table of Contents

Remembrance

Somewhere in my memories of childhood, I can still see my young fingers fighting with a pair of scissors in my determination to cut out the orange-and-blue illustration of Sam Snead's face from the back of a box of Wheaties. In the days before television, a picture on a cereal box amounted to a media coup. So I gleefully added The Slammer to my burgeoning collection of trading cards. And I became a fan of golf.

My next golf awakening came in the spring of my sophomore year of high school when I found myself swept up in the unfolding fortunes of Arnold Palmer. I also watched as a young cub began his climb to become a Golden Bear and witnessed a hotshot out of West Texas, with Mexico in his veins, blister the tour in the late 1960s and early '70s.

In 1972, a Music City songwriter named Joe Allen gave me a set of H&Bs, took me to a driving range, and loaned me Ben Hogan's bible, *Five Lessons*. Joe firmly convinced me that we're never too old to learn the game of golf.

Twenty-four years later — during which time countless gifted athletes paved the way for golf's next generation — I experienced the warm pleasure of playing my first-ever round with my two sons. The Great Fraternity had enclosed itself around more innocent prey. And the Great Wheel rolls on.

Introduction

It isn't often that one has the opportunity to step back with perspective and look with pride upon a major contribution his family has made to the quality of life everywhere. In this instance, my family, I feel, should rightfully take its exalted place atop golf's great names: Jones, Hogan, Nicklaus ... Ross? Yes, Ross!

You won't find our surname at the top of any leaderboard, past or present, but players everywhere may have the Rosses, and a few of their friends, to thank for the game of golf today.

Back in the 15th century, Scotland's King James II prohibitively banned golf throughout the kingdom. The game was viewed as evil and a distraction to the crown's loftier goals at the time — killing its citizens in a relentless series of on-going battles, as well as defending its shores from legitimate outside aggressors. But Clan Ross, together with the Crawfords, independent Highlanders that they were, raised an army in 1452 and set out to overthrow James II. Though the rebel charge was defeated by the King's men at Brechin, a message loud and clear was issued that day that has reverberated through the centuries — even a king lacks the power to come between avid golfers and their tee times. Of course, the links ban was lifted.

But now, let's return to the present ...

As a writer and fan, I am always interested whenever a modern athlete makes reference to the history of his or her sport. Unfortunately, these references are all too rare.

Historical perspective puts each game into a broader framework that carries more meaning than simply hitting a ball, kicking a ball, catching a ball or throwing a ball. Sports history is about heroes and character, headlines and characters. It's about embracing the great performances that stand for a time and are then surpassed.

Once in a great while, a feat goes untouched through the ages: Joe DiMaggio's 56-game hitting streak in 1941, Ernie Nevers' 40 points scored in a single NFL game in 1929, Bobby Jones' momentous golfing Grand Slam in 1930. It is all, still, such wonder to me. The beckoning to the game through the achievements of others is, for me, the essence of an on-going love affair with sports.

On the pages that follow, I've attempted to tell, albeit in abbreviated form, the essential history of the ancient game of golf. Hopefully, this story, along with its marvelous cast of characters, will entertain and educate those who love the game enough to learn more about its past. And now, with no further introductions necessary, lets tee it up ... whether the king likes it, or not.

Chapter 1

ORIGINS:
GOLF'S BEGINNINGS

The Scot comes in from his best-ever round. The man on the veranda says to him, "Well, how'd you do today?" He answers, "Not bad."

We fear that boastfulness can anger the gods.

John Gilchrist,
former provost of St. Andrews

Country First

The mid-15th century is recognized as a time establishing the first tangible evidence that golf was being played in Scotland. And odd evidence it is: a document indicating that Scottish Parliament was *banning* the game of Golfe, as well as Fute-ball!

It seems the two pastimes were disrupting Scotsmen from a more serious endeavor at the time: the defense of their country from the kingdom's enemies.

Though there is some disagreement as to whether the Dutch or the Scottish first founded the game of golf, no one disputes St. Andrews, lying by the North Sea on the east coast of Scotland, as the cradle of golf.

St. Andrews

Venerable, world-renowned St. Andrews is widely accepted as the world's first full-length outdoor golf course. But its date of origin is a matter of debate, with some historians dating it back as early as the 12th century. This much seems certain: The governing organization at St. Andrews — the Royal and Ancient Club — wasn't officially chartered till the year 1754.

Gutta-Percha

The first golf balls were made of feathers packed into hand-stitched leather, and, in the mid 1800s, were sold in Scottish golf shops for half a crown. But in 1848, the juice from the gutta-percha tree helped form a gummy substance that made the ball travel further when hit. *And* it was far less expensive than the "feathery." The gutta-percha ball, extolled by Old Tom Morris (see page 23), soon established its superiority and ushered in a new age in golf.

The Haskell Ball

A rubber-cored ball that added an extra 20 yards on the average drive was created by an amateur Cleveland golfer named Coburn Haskell and developed in conjunction with the Goodrich Rubber Company in 1902. It soon made the gutta-percha ball obsolete.

Ye Olde Clubs

The modern numbering of golf clubs was not universally adopted until the 1940s. Before then, a colorful 19th century Scottish vocabulary existed for the names of the various clubs.

- Driver: 1-wood or driver
- Brassie: 2-wood
- Spoon: 3-wood
- Driving cleek: 1-iron
- Mid iron: 2-iron
- Mid mashie: 3-iron
- Mashie iron: 4-iron
- Mashie: 5-iron
- Spade mashie: 6-iron
- Mashie niblick: 7-iron
- Niblick: 8-9 iron/wedge
- Super niblick: Sand wedge

The Father of American Golf

Transplanted Scotlander John Reid, certain that golf would be a "remarkable sport because it was a Scottish sport," hand-scooped three "cups" out of the ground in a pasture in Yonkers, NY, on George Washington's Birthday, 1888. It was there that Reid, along with playing partner, John B. Upton, played the first game of golf on American soil.

Reid also founded the first golf course in America, St. Andrew's. The course began on that three-hole field in Yonkers and changed locations four times in its first 10 years.

St. Andrew's carries the same name (though distinguished by an apostrophe) as its illustrious predecessor in Scotland — the world's first course. The U.S. namesake is located in Ardsley, New York.

The First Great Golfers

Young Tom Morris won four British Opens consecutively, from 1868 through 1872 (no championship was held in 1871). His brilliant career was cut short by death at the age of 24, from heartbreak, after the death of his wife and newborn child.

His father, Old Tom Morris, one of early golf's greatest players/supporters/promoters/architects also won four British Opens — all in the 1860s.

First U.S. Amateur Championship

Twenty players teed off at Newport, Rhode Island's Rocky Farm course in September of 1894. Heavily favored Chicagoan, Charles Blair Macdonald, took a four-stroke lead into the final round of medal play but lost the championship on a two-stroke penalty, allotted when his ball lodged into one of the course's meandering stone walls, to W. G. Lawrence of Newport Golf Club.

First *Official* U.S. Amateur Championship

After two losses in the first two amateur championships, Macdonald, the best golfer in America in the early 1890s, won the first "official" U.S. Amateur Championship, sponsored by the USGA, at Newport, in October 1895.

USGA

The U.S. Golf Association was formed on Dec. 22, 1894, when delegates from five of the country's most prestigious golf clubs met at the Calumet Club in New York to "promote the interests of the game of golf, to promulgate a code of rules for the game, and to schedule competitions for the amateur and open championships in the United States."

Walter J. Travis

The first great American golfer was Walter J. Travis, a late bloomer who did not pick up a club till his mid-thirties. Though born in Australia, Travis is considered an American golfer, having moved to the United States as a young boy and having learned the game here. Less than four years after taking up golf at age 35, he won the 1900 U. S. Amateur Championship. He would win two of the next three national amateurs — three in four years.

But more importantly, Travis elevated American golf to the international level when, in 1904, he astounded the world with his domination of the British Amateur Championship, the first foreigner to ever wrest the title from the native Scots and Britons.

World War I

During World War I, no official U.S. Amateur or Open championships were held, but exhibitions to raise money for the war effort were everywhere. Among the participating stars were Walter Hagen, Francis Ouimet, Chick Evans, and a young 15-year-old who made the tough game of golf look, literally, like child's play — Bobby Jones, Jr. Women also toured in the exhibitions, including a young U.S. women's champion, Alexa Stirling.

In all, millions of dollars were raised and, through the concerted efforts and generosity of the unselfish stars, America began to look upon golf with a new-found respect and admiration. During 1918, Evans, who was one of America's premier golfers immediately preceding the war, single-handedly raised close to $300,000, traveling over 26,000 miles with appearances in 41 cities.

Chapter 2

THE 15 GREATEST GOLFERS OF ALL TIME

15.

Greg Norman

An all-time leading career money winner on the PGA Tour, "The Shark" is considered one of the greatest golfers of the last quarter century. Norman's record (50-plus international wins plus over a dozen PGA victories) entitles him to be classified as a great global star. Unfortunately, Norman has been plagued by numerous final-round collapses and a spate of second-place finishes. He has lost playoffs in all four majors; his collapse in the last round of the 1996 Masters is regarded as near tragic. Still, Greg Norman has garnered two major championships (both British Opens) and has the consolation of having been *shown* the money. Lots of it.

14.

Lee Trevino

The loquacious Super Mex ranks among golf's all-time greats, not only for the excellence of his game, but also for his colorful personality. A commanding competitor, Trevino made a big splash coming out of West Texas to join the PGA Tour in 1967, when he was named Rookie of the Year. In all, he won 27 PGA Tour victories, including six majors — two U.S. Opens, two PGAs, and two British Opens. He was the tour's leading money winner in 1970 and its Player of the Year in 1971. Trevino has been a major force on the Senior PGA Tour too, claiming 27 wins in his first seven years on the circuit.

All men are created free and equal, and I am one shot better than the rest.

Gene Sarazen's credo

Gene Sarazen in his seventies still made golf look so simple.

Henry Longhurst

13.

Gene Sarazen

The only man who successfully contested the great Walter Hagen in the 1920s, Sarazen is best remembered for his stunning double-eagle in the 1935 Masters that enabled him to tie, then defeat, Craig Wood in a playoff. He is the first player to ever log a career modern Grand Slam and won seven major titles, including three PGA Championships. In 1973, at the grand old age of 71, Sarazen wowed the world when he aced the infamous "Postage Stamp" hole at Royal Troon in the golden anniversary celebration of his first appearance in the British Open.

His forte: a big, if somewhat errant driver and an approach-shot *afficion.*

Roger Matuz,
on Severiano Ballesteros

There is no "jail" from which Ballesteros cannot escape.

Robin McMillan

12.

Seve Ballesteros

The brilliant Spanish shotmaker won a mere six tournaments as a touring PGA golfer, but that's because he preferred to play in Europe for the majority of his career. He had victories on four continents before his 21st birthday and, at age 23, became the youngest Masters champion up to that time.

One of the games' great long-iron hitters, Ballesteros holds five major championship titles, including three wins in the British Open. He is said to favor Arnold Palmer and Walter Hagen with his inventive shotmaking.

He is a kid among men, and he is showing the men how to play.

Tom Watson,
on Tiger Woods

11.

Tiger Woods

Tiger Woods has the look of a champion and the potential to become golf's greatest player ever. Coming off a brilliant amateur career, where he won an unprecedented three straight U.S. Amateur Championships, Woods stormed onto the professional circuit in late 1996 and won two of the first seven events in which he played. During that seven-tournament run, he registered a breathtaking 14 eagles.

But Tiger's most impressive moment was still ahead. In his first major championship as a pro, Woods broke a slew of long-esteemed records in the prestigious Masters, in 1997, including carding an unbelievable 18-under par for the tournament and winning by the largest margin ever — 12 strokes.

I don't see how *anyone* can beat him.

> *Mike Turnesa,*
> *PGA touring pro caught*
> *in the maelstrom of Byron Nelson's*
> *11-consecutive victory tornado in 1945*

10.

Byron Nelson

Lord Byron separated himself from the pack by placing in the money in 113 consecutive tournaments in 1944 and '45. He won an unimaginable 11 consecutive PGA tour events in 1945 — a streak akin to Joe DiMaggio's baseball mark of hitting safely in 56 straight games. His 18 wins in a single year (19 if you count the San Francisco Open which ran from December 1944 into January of '45) is a PGA record. Nelson also recorded two Masters triumphs, one U.S. Open championship and three PGA crowns in the major tournaments, 54 victories in all.

For Arnold Palmer, it's let it go or let it blow —
all or nothing.

Nathaniel Avery,
onetime Palmer caddy

If I ever needed an eight-foot putt and everything
I owned depended on it, I would want Arnold Palmer
to putt it for me.

Bobby Jones, Jr.

9.

Arnold Palmer

The most popular golfer of all time, the legendary Arnold Palmer, complete with his own army of adoring zealots, first brought the game to the masses. The rise of television, juxtaposed with Palmer's own rise, lifted the popularity of the sport to its current heights. The patented Palmer "charge" became a household word, as Arnie surged to 1960 Masters and U.S. Open victories in highly dramatic fashion. The legend was launched. Palmer would claim eight major tournaments during his storied career on his way to 60 official PGA Tour wins, fourth on the all-time list.

Tomorrow you're going to see a small miracle. In fact, you're going to see a large miracle. I'm going to win the British Open.

Gary Player,
to a friend on the eve of the final 36 holes
of the 1959 British Open at Muirfield —
eight strokes off the pace.
He won by two.

8.

Gary Player

The likable Man in Black secured his legendary stature in the annals of golf with his commanding performances in the major championships. Though only registering 21 victories on the PGA Tour, Player took nine of golf's major crowns back home to Johannesburg, South Africa, including three British Opens and three Masters. In addition, he won more than 120 tournaments internationally. Player is one of only four golfers ever to have won a career modern Grand Slam. The others are Gene Sarazen, Jack Nicklaus and Ben Hogan.

H e took them through all the emotions. He would play a succession of holes as though divinely inspired, while they marveled at his skill. Then from a clear sky would come a stroke of unbelievable inaccuracy — a wild slice, or a top, or a quick, semi-circular hook — and the heart of the duffer warmed to the god that could descend to the level of man.

Henry Longhurst,
on Walter Hagen

7.

Walter Hagen

A blend of colorful personality and inscrutable skill, Walter Hagen was a formidable presence on golf's sweeping stage for well over two decades. Among his notable achievements, "The Haig" claimed two U.S. Opens, four British Open crowns, and five PGA titles, easily qualifying him as America's first dominant professional golfer.

Considered golf's greatest showman, Hagen was a gallery charmer who had a knack for the dramatic and who could often find poise in the face of pending disaster. In later years, his love for the party life took its toll on his game.

6.

Tom Watson

Hardworking Tom Watson will always be remembered for his dramatic recovery shot from the deep rough off the 17th green at Pebble Beach in the 1982 U.S. Open. Holing out a chip shot from that difficult lie immortalized Watson, who went on to defeat Jack Nicklaus for his only U.S. Open title.

But Watson's place in history is secure for his phenomenal five victories in the British Open, tied for second all-time behind the legendary Harry Vardon's six triumphs. In all, Watson is the holder of over 30 PGA Tour victories, including eight majors. Only the PGA championship has eluded him in his quest for a career Grand Slam.

He is a six-time PGA Player of the Year and was elected into the World Golf Hall of Fame in 1988.

5.

Harry Vardon

The master, Harry Vardon, an Englishman and six-time winner of the British Open (the world's most prestigious tournament in modern golf's early era), took the 1900 U.S. Open at Chicago Country Club as part of a nationwide tour sponsored by the A. G. Spalding Company to promote its new golf ball, the Vardon Flyer.

Vardon, regarded through the first 75 years of the 20th Century as one of the four greatest golfers of all time, had such consistency in his graceful swing that opponents swore when he played the second nine holes over a nine-hole course, his shots would fall into the divot marks he'd made on the fairways his first time around.

All the world loves a long hitter, and Sam Snead could really powder that apple. His shots were far more beautiful than the raving sportswriters had claimed they were. Watching him, like watching Jones, provided an aesthetic delight.

Herbert Warren Wind

4.

Sam Snead

The Slammer ranks No. 1 all-time in career PGA wins with 81. Snead also set records for tour longevity, playing in five decades and becoming the first PGA Tour player in history to shoot his age or better with rounds of 67 and 66 in the 1979 Quad Cities Open.

He also became the oldest golfer, at 52, ever to win a regular PGA event, when he took the Greater Greensboro Open a record eighth time. Just as Jack Nicklaus rivaled Arnold Palmer in the 1960s and '70s, Snead staged a series of memorable clashes throughout the 1940s and '50s with arch nemesis Ben Hogan.

During his brilliant career, Slammin' Sam garnered seven major tournament victories. Only one major eluded him. Thus Snead may also be remembered as the best player never to win the U.S. Open.

Ben Hogan was the greatest golfer you ever dreamed of seeing. Arnold Palmer and Jack Nicklaus are great. But listen, they couldn't carry Ben's jock-strap. Only way you beat Ben was if God wanted you to.

Tommy Bolt

3.

Ben Hogan

"The Hawk" is considered one of the greatest players of all time. Steel-eyed and steel-nerved, Hogan ruled golf, along with Sam Snead, in the 1940s and early '50s. A horrific head-on car crash with a bus in early 1949 nearly took his life, but the irrepressible Bantam Ben came back miraculously the following year to win the 1950 U.S. Open and then went on to claim five *additional* major titles. In 1953, having won the Masters, U.S. Open and British Open, Hogan's once-in-a-lifetime chance at golf's Grand Slam was squelched by a scheduling mishap: the British Open and PGA Championship happened to overlap that year.

I have found only one sports figure who could stand up in every way as a gentleman as well as a celebrity; a fine, decent human being as well as a newsprint personage, and one who never once since I have known him has let me down in my estimate of him.

Paul Gallico,
on Bobby Jones, Jr.

There is a strain of poetry about Bobby Jones.

Bernard Darwin,
legendary British golf writer

Golf without Bobby Jones is like France without Paris.

Herbert Warren Wind,
on Jones' retirement announcement
in late 1930

2.

Bobby Jones, Jr.

From the time he first appeared on the tournament scene as a 14-year-old phenom, Robert Tyre Jones, Jr., better known as Bobby Jones, was predicted to win championships by all who saw him. The chubby Atlantan with the graceful swing would, in time, take 13 major titles — more than any man in the history of the game other than Jack Nicklaus. Though he was the nonpareil of the era, amateur or professional, it would take him 11 tries before he would claim his first national championship, the 1923 U.S. Open.

The brilliant Jones dominated the amateur field in his time, due in large part to the exodus of the better golfers to the pro ranks. Yet he overwhelmed the leading professionals of the day as well. His epic milestone in the game still stands: the only man ever to win golf's Grand Slam in the same year. That incomparable feat, achieved in 1930, included the U.S. and British Amateur Championships along with the U.S. and British Opens.

1.

Jack Nicklaus

Jack is playing an entirely different game — a game I'm not even familiar with.

Bobby Jones, Jr.,
on the power golf of young Jack Nicklaus,
in 1965.

He is considered by most players, writers, fans and analysts to be the greatest golfer who ever played the game. Among his record 20 major tournament wins, the Golden Bear displayed a fondness for the Masters, claiming a stunning six green blazers. He is also a five-time winner of the PGA Championship, four-time victor in the U.S. Open, and three-time British Open champion.

Nicklaus amassed 70 PGA Tour wins after turning pro in 1962. As a dominating amateur at Ohio State, the big Bear won an NCAA title in 1961 and two U.S. Amateur Championships in 1959 and '61. As a senior, Nicklaus has ten Senior Tour wins.

In addition to his unparalleled play, the Golden Bear has earned a well-deserved reputation as one of the world's great golf-course architects.

Chapter 3

THE MAJORS

In the era of Bobby Jones, the Grand Slam was comprised of the Amateur and Open titles from both America and Great Britain. Today, the modern slam is made up of four major tournaments — the Masters, U.S. Open, British Open and PGA Championship — although the U.S. Amateur is still viewed as a major title and counts in a golfer's major tournament total.

The Masters

The Masters is a heavyweight championship fight that lasts four days. It's the horses in the gates at the Kentucky Derby.

Anonymous player's agent

Inaugurated in 1934, the Masters is the only one of the four majors that is stationary, being played annually on the private and sumptuous grounds of Augusta National in Augusta, Georgia. The course was co-designed by Dr. Alister Mackenzie and Bobby Jones, Jr. and is considered one of the premier tests of golf in the world.

Horton Smith, the Joplin Ghost, won two of the first three Masters titles, from 1934-36. Augusta National, infamous for its Amen Corner — the 11th, 12th and 13th holes — has taken the zing out of a lot of swings over the years. A thoroughly flabbergasted Lee Trevino once held a news conference to announce his intention to never again attempt to tame Augusta National, thereby jettisoning his only remaining opportunity to earn a career Grand Slam.

Its winning trophy is unique in sport — a green blazer sports jacket that signifies a very elite organization: not just the membership at Augusta National Golf Club but the roll call of greats who have won the Masters tournament.

The Five Greatest
Masters Tournaments

Honorable Mention

1968 — Tommy Aaron's clerical blunder costs Roberto de Vicenzo a playoff with Bob Goalby for The Jacket. De Vicenzo signs an incorrect scorecard (Aaron had recorded a 4 on 17, where de Vicenzo had actually shot a birdie 3), thereby handing the Masters outright to Goalby.

1987 — Larry Mize holes out a 50-yard pitch-and-run on the second playoff hole to beat Greg Norman and Seve Ballesteros for the Green.

5.

1935 — The Most Famous Double-Eagle
in History

Gene Sarazen's astonishing double-eagle on the 15th hole forces a playoff with Craig Wood. Sarazen breezes in the 36-hole playoff, winning the second-ever Masters by five strokes.

4.

1996 — Back Door Man

Greg Norman's final-round six-stroke collapse allows Nick Faldo in the back door to the green jacket fitting room.

3.

1960 — The Charge Heard 'Round
the World

Arnold Palmer's birdie-birdie finish beats Ken Venturi by a stroke. This first-ever televised display of a Palmer closing charge energizes Arnie's Army.

2.

1986 — Jack Nicklaus Wins Record Sixth Masters and 20th Major Tournament at Age 46

This was the sentimental choice for No. 1, understandably — after all, a sixth green jacket and a 20th major in one's golden years doesn't happen *every* April.

1.

1997 — Tiger Woods Masters Augusta National

It isn't enough that he is playing in just his first Masters as a professional and wins. He wins big — *real* big. A lot of legends of golf have played and won at Augusta, but *no one* ever won by 12 strokes, with a four-day total of 270, 18 below par.

U.S. Open

Less than a year after the formulation of the United States Golf Association, the first U.S. Open was held, in 1895, at the ritzy nine-hole spread of the Newport Golf Club in Rhode Island.

A Scotsman named Willie Anderson dominated the early 1900s, taking four Opens in five years. The most venerable and prestigious of the American majors, the U.S. Open has a grand foursome heading its annals in number of championships won — Anderson, Bobby Jones, Ben Hogan and Jack Nicklaus all own four Open titles apiece.

The Five Greatest U.S. Opens

Honorable Mention

1973 — Johnny Miller's final-round 63 at Oakmont sets a U.S. Open record and erases a daunting six-stroke deficit, in claiming the first of his two major-tournament wins.

1955 — With Ben Hogan already announced as the winner on TV and his "winning" ball having just been presented to the USGA Golf Museum, unknown Jack Fleck runs a birdie string to tie Hogan and force a playoff at the Olympic Club in San Francisco. Fleck whips The Hawk by three strokes in the playoff.

5.

1966 — Casper Snatches Open Crown from Palmer

Billy Casper comes from an impossible seven strokes back with just nine holes to play to beat a reeling Arnold Palmer at Olympic in San Francisco for his second U.S. Open crown.

4.

1913 — Unknown Is First Amateur to Win Open Title

20-year-old amateur Francis Ouimet ousts two renowned British golfers, including the great Harry Vardon, in an 18-hole playoff at Brookline to put America on the world golfing map.

3.

1960 — Arnie Marches On in Big Year

Arnold Palmer charges again to win his second major in a row, coming from seven strokes behind on the final day, at Cherry Hills outside Denver, to claim his one and only U.S. Open championship.

2.

1923 — Gutsy Shot Brings Jones First National Championship

Bobby Jones, Jr. takes his first national title, beating scrappy Bobby Cruickshank on the last playoff hole with a daring 2-iron approach shot from the rough that covers 190 yards and carries a lagoon fronting the green at 18, at Inwood (Long Island) Country Club.

1.

1962 — Nicklaus vs. Palmer: First Duel

A young Jack Nicklaus defeats reigning tour superstar Arnold Palmer by three strokes in an 18-hole playoff. Making the victory sweeter is the tournament's whereabouts: at Oakmont, in the heart of Palmer country.

The British Open

The granddaddy of them all, this linksland major originated way back in 1860. On the windswept open countryside of coastal Scotland, Old Tom Morris and his son, Young Tom, created their respective legends, taming the ubiquitous whins, winding burns and impossible winds on their way to claiming eight of the first 12 British Opens.

But it's the old master, Harry Vardon, better known for his universal "Vardon Grip" — the overlap position of the hands in gripping a club — who is king of the British Open titleholders, with six. Lagging just one championship behind, with five crowns each, are Australian banger Peter Thomson, American great Tom Watson, and J. H. Taylor and James Braid from the turn of the 20th century.

The Five Greatest British Opens

Honorable Mention

1870 — The legendary Young Tom Morris murders Prestwick Course, including scoring a two on the 578-yard first hole. He wins the Open by twelve strokes.

1970 — Jack Nicklaus drives the 358-yard finishing hole at St. Andrews for his second British Open crown. He drove it all four rounds of the tournament.

1896 — Harry Vardon claims the first of his record six Open titles in a playoff against ultimate five-time British Open winner, J. H. Taylor.

5.

1972 — Phenomenal Third-Round Recovery Shots Bring Trevino Title

At Muirfield, having pushed his approach at 16 into a bunker 30 feet from the cup, Lee Trevino miraculously holes out. On the 17th, he saves par by stroking in from just off the edge of the green. The rally would lead to his second Open win in a row.

4.

1922 — Hagen Becomes First American to Win British Open

Using one of his patented impossible recovery shots, Walter Hagen chips from the sand on the 15th hole at Sandwich to within a foot of the cup for the momentum needed to break the British stranglehold on the Open.

3.

1926 — Bobby Jones' Prodigious Sand Blast Locks Up Open

Tied for the lead heading to 17 at Royal Lytham and St. Annes in the final round, Jones' drive finds unraked sand at the corner of the dogleg left. Hitting a four-iron, his ball lands on the green 175 yards away and holds. That shot, commemorated with a plaque near the spot where it was hit, carries Jones to the first of three British Open titles.

2.

1953 — Ben Hogan Claims Triple Crown with Win at Carnoustie

Only four years removed from his near-fatal car crash, Hogan, battling the flu and ill weather, marches relentlessly through the final day's 36 holes to win the Open in his only attempt. It is also the last jewel in his remarkable 1953 Triple Crown, when he won the Masters and U.S. Open, in addition to the British Open.

1.

1977 — Watson Ekes by Nicklaus at Turnberry

Some have hailed it as the greatest head-to-head matchup in golf history. Shooting identical 68s, 70s, and 65s the first three rounds, Jack Nicklaus and Tom Watson continue their extraordinary play into the fourth round. Back and forth the lead goes, with both pulling matching birdies on 18, but Watson wins it by one.

PGA Championship

Calendar-wise, the PGA is the fourth leg of the Slam. Originating in 1916, it has achieved a certain infamy over the years for being the one tournament that both Arnold Palmer and Tom Watson have failed to win, thereby excluding the two legends from the so-called "career" Grand Slam club. And of course, it is the major that yielded a record four consecutive times in the mid-'20s to the imperturbable Walter Hagen. The tournament was a match-play affair up until 1968, when the event changed to strokeplay. Hagen and Jack Nicklaus are joint leaders in championships won, with five each.

The Five Greatest PGA Championships

Honorable Mention

1928 — Leo Diegel snaps Walter Hagen's eternal mark of 22 straight wins in PGA Championship match play, in the quarterfinals, and beats two-time PGA champ Gene Sarazen in the semifinals en route to his first of two back-to-back PGA Championship crowns.

1930 — Tommy Armour, the "Silver Scot," defeats Gene Sarazen at Five Farms (MD) on the final putt of the final hole, after mirroring each other stroke for stroke in their 36-hole match-play final.

5.

1991 — Real Life "Tin Cup" Win for Daly

Everybody's favorite golf movie comes to life for then-unknown John Daly. The long Crooked Stick course suits his game, and Daly never buckles under major tournament pressure.

4.

1972 — Recovery Shot Sews Up Player's Second PGA Championship

Having let a final-round three-stroke lead evaporate by the 16th hole at Oakland Hills, Gary Player mishits his drive into thick, wet rough. Worse still, the ball lies behind a willow-tree stand. Player selects a 9-iron and powers the ball just over the tip of the willows. It lands four feet from the cup. Ball game.

3.

1986 — Tway's Bunker Shot Shoots Down The Shark

Entering the final nine holes at Inverness with a four-stroke lead, Greg Norman is tied by Bob Tway with one hole to go. Tway finds rough, then a bunker; Norman is just off the green in two. But Fate again hands Norman a staggering defeat when Tway holes his improbable blast from the sand.

2.

1969 — Boros Beats Time and an Army

It is better known as the PGA Championship that Arnold Palmer lost — the one Grand Slam event he failed to win in his sterling career. Palmer, heading into 18 down by a stroke, blasts a Herculean 230-yard 3-wood from the rough to within eight feet of the cup. But Julius Boros counters with his trademark excellent short game and wins by a stroke when Palmer misses his tying putt. For Boros, the win earns him the distinction of being the oldest golfer ever to win a major (48 years, 4 months).

1.

1927 — Hagen Wins Fourth Consecutive PGA Championship

The peerless master of match play, Walter Hagen has been tested in the early rounds and even employs some psychological gamesmanship to his advantage in the semifinals. His opponent, Joe Turnesa, lapses towards the end of the match. Needing to sink his potential tournament-tying putt on the match's final hole, Turnesa leaves it at the cup's lip. Hagen has won his fourth straight PGA Championship.

During the sweltering last nine holes at Cedar Crest in Dallas, Hagen is given a hat to wear by a young 15-year-old spectator named Byron Nelson, who would one day become a two-time winner of the PGA.

Chapter 4

THE 15 GREATEST MOMENTS IN GOLF HISTORY

15.

Impossible Double-Eagle Catapults Sarazen to 1935 Masters Crown

Down three strokes to the prolific Craig Wood with just four holes to play in the 1935 Masters, Gene Sarazen eyes his second shot on the par-5 15th at Augusta, then 485 yards long. Taking first a three-wood, then switching to a 4-wood, Sarazen unloads toward the flag, 235 yards away. The blast carries the pond in front of the green and lands on the green's front section. The shot has eagle possibilities as it continues its path on a line for the pin. But the ball seems destined for the hole itself, as if it were being reeled in. It hits nothing but cup. The elated Sarazen has made up the three strokes on one unbelievable hole. Some golf experts have called it the most sensational shot in golf history. Sarazen goes on to beat Wood by five strokes in a 36-hole playoff the following day.

14.

Snead vs. Hogan — 1954 Masters Playoff

It was one of golf's greatest rivalries — the sweet-swinging Slammer from Hot Springs, Virginia, versus the machine-like Bantam from Ft. Worth, Texas. Throughout the 1940s and early '50s, these two titans of the game gave golf its earliest big-name rivalry, with the possible exception, for a time, of Walter Hagen and Gene Sarazen. The Snead-Hogan duels would pave the way for golf's next major head-on clash — the Arnold Palmer-Jack Nicklaus shootouts of the 1960s.

Now late in their collective prime, Snead and Hogan end the final round of the 1954 Masters tied. Earlier that day, Hogan actually is more concerned with catching a young hot amateur named Billy Joe Patton. Misinformed about Patton's performance, Hogan, then at the beginning of the notorious Amen Corner, presses and winds up double-bogeying the 11th. He would finish one stroke ahead of Patton but only manage to tie Snead, already in the clubhouse. In the following day's 18-hole playoff, Hogan's drives lack their trademark fade, and Bantam Ben loses the green jacket by a stroke to his longtime nemesis.

13.

Watson's Astonishing Recovery Takes 1982 U.S. Open

Locked in a tight duel with the formidable Jack Nicklaus in the 1982 U.S. Open at Pebble Beach, Tom Watson goes into the par-3 17th in the final round deadlocked with the Golden Bear. Off the 17th tee, Watson hooks a 2-iron into thick rough. What happened next is considered one of the greatest recovery shots under pressure in modern golfing history. Lying hole-high and eight feet from the green's fringe, Watson takes a sand wedge, opening the blade, and cuts under and just across the ball. It hits the edge of the green and rolls the next 12 feet in a slight curve from right to left. It hits the pin dead center and sinks into the cup. Watson pars the 18th to win his only U.S. Open.

12.

Palmer vs. Nicklaus — at 20 Paces

Hailed as the finest amateur since Bobby Jones, young Ohio State star Jack Nicklaus had already served notice of his staggering abilities, having won two U.S. Amateurs. But in 1962, without any new worlds to conquer, Nicklaus turned pro.

Two years earlier, as a precocious amateur, Nicklaus had come within a stroke of winning the U.S. Open — the year Arnold Palmer made his storied final-round charge. Now, at famed Oakmont on the outskirts of Pittsburgh, Palmer enjoys a near-hometown advantage, sweeping into the final round with a two-stroke lead. But young Jack ties the popular Palmer to force an 18-hole playoff. Palmer starts horrendously, falling off the pace four strokes in six holes. Though he charges to within a stroke, Palmer three-putts the 13th. They match pars the rest of the way, but Nicklaus wins with a comfortable three-stroke margin. A famous rivalry is born.

11.

Ken Venturi's Brave 1964 U.S. Open Win

The Ken Venturi story is a saga of unlimited promise followed by heartbreaking defeats, slumps, and mounting injuries for most of his career. But on a mid-June weekend in 1964, Venturi put on one of the most courageous exhibitions of guts and golf in the long history of the sport.

Entering the final double-round at Congressional, just outside Washington, DC, Venturi begins to wilt from exhaustion due to the day's heat. Lying down between rounds and walking the final 18 holes with a doctor by his side, he manages to produce enough winning shots to take the Open title by four strokes. Some have called it the most stirring national championship since Francis Ouimet beat the two British stars in the 1913 Open.

10.

Bobby Jones' All-or-Nothing Shot Wins 1923 U.S. Open Playoff

Holding a three-stroke lead as final-round play begins in the 1923 U.S. Open at Inwood Country Club on Long Island, 21-year-old Bobby Jones, Jr. looks like he might be on the verge of winning his first major tournament.

But a bogey, bogey, double-bogey finish leaves him backing into the win at best. His competition, Bobby Cruickshank, offers no compliance under the circumstances, fighting to par then birdie the last two holes in regulation to tie Jones and force a playoff.

"Well, I didn't finish like a champion," Jones remarks. "I finished like a yellow dog." But the playoff presents him with the opportunity for redemption.

Back and forth they go in the following day's playoff, exchanging the lead until, after 17 holes, they are again tied dead even. Jones' drive on 18 leaves him with a poor lie in loose dirt just off the fairway. A lagoon lies just before the green, 200 yards away. Jones then unleashes one of the most dramatic shots in golf history — a drilled 2-iron that carries the lagoon and comes to rest six feet from the cup. "The Emperor" has his first major championship and achieves it like a champion.

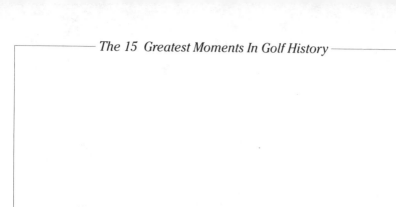

It's what I do. My tee shots allow me to position myself on the greens for eagles and birdies.

Tiger Woods

9.

Tiger Takes Unprecedented Third Straight U. S. Amateur

Only one golfer in history has ever recorded his fourth major tournament win in his first full season as a professional. Don't forget that the U.S. Amateur is considered a major. So when that child prodigy, Tiger Woods, detonated Augusta National in the spring of 1997 for his fourth major title, golf fans knew they were witnessing something special. From 1994 through '96, Woods did something no amateur golfer, not even the legendary Bobby Jones, had ever done — Tiger won three consecutive U.S. Amateurs.

His last win is accomplished in spectacular style. Down an impossible five holes beginning the final round, Woods whittles away at University of Florida sophomore Steve Scott's lead. Tiger ties the match, holing a magnificent 35-foot birdie putt on 17, and wins the playoff a history-making third time.

8.

Palmer's Rocky Mountain High

Arnold Palmer, the young lion king of golf at age 29, comes into the 1960 U.S. Open at Cherry Hills (south of Denver, Colorado) a strong favorite, having started off the season by winning four winter tournaments, topped by his second Masters victory in April. A distant eight strokes behind leader Mike Souchak going into the final day, Palmer begins another memorable "charge" that will soon spawn a legend. Playing the then-customary 36 holes on the Open's last day, Arnie is still down seven strokes with just 18 holes to play. He cans a torrid six birdies in seven holes on the front nine, going out at the turn in 30 — five strokes below par. He wins going away, by two strokes; the General and his Army are born.

7.

Ouimet's Victory in 1913 U.S. Open Elevates American Golf

In 1913, vaunted English golfers Harry Vardon and Ted Ray toured America in a series of exhibitions. It was Vardon's second trip to the States. They interrupted their tour long enough to participate in the U.S. Open at Brookline. The Open that year would be a big test for American golf, which was attempting to raise its stature against the more established European stars.

A local 20-year-old from Brookline, Francis Ouimet, rises from the ranks of the unknown to stun the two British stars in an unforgettable playoff, after the three finish regular play deadlocked in an improbable tie. Though he would never win another Open, Ouimet remains a mainstay in American amateur ranks until the Bobby Jones era. In 1931, 17 years after he had beaten rival Jerry Travers for his first U.S. Amateur title, Ouimet, an old man at 38, wins a second amateur championship.

It's a shame Bob Jones isn't here now. He could have saved the words for me in '63 for this young man, because he's *certainly* playing a game we're not familiar with.

Jack Nicklaus,
on Tiger Woods

6.

Woods Eats Up Augusta in '97 Masters

The 61st Masters began as a tutorial for young Tiger Woods. His first encounter of Augusta National as a professional (he'd played before as an amateur but not too successfully) started shakily with a stratospheric 40 on the front nine. But by the end of the fourth round, it had become an eloquent golfing tutorial *by* Woods.

The clinic officially began with a zone-like 30 on the inbound nine that first day to salvage a 70. Awe-inspiring rounds of 66, 65 and the closing 69 brought him in at a staggering 18-under par, a new tournament record, as was the 12-point margin of victory. In fact only our friend, Old Tom Morris, the four-time British Open winner and promoter of the old gutta-percha ball, won a major tournament — the 1862 British Open — by a greater margin: 13 strokes. In all, Woods broke or tied nine Masters records, including youngest winner. The famous green jacket never had a better fit.

He makes more bad shots in a single season than Harry Vardon did during the whole period in which he won six British Open championships. But he beats more immaculate golfers because three of "those" and one of "them" counts four, and he knows it.

Arthur Croome,
The Morning Post,
on Walter Hagen

He makes such odd shots from the tee — and he takes so few shots about the green! He can be so shockingly wild and so distressingly precise, all playing the same hole! He's the great match golfer, is Sir Walter!

O. B. Keeler

Hagen could make tying his shoelaces seem more dramatic than the other guy's hole-in-one.

Herbert Warren Wind

5.

Hagen's Illustrious Quad

With most of golf's literati ready to eulogize him, the great Walter Hagen adds still another remarkable laurel to his bejeweled crown as pro golf's main man of the 1910s and '20s. Having grabbed three successive PGA Championships from 1924-26, Hagen adds an improbable fourth title in Dallas in 1927. The master of match play, Hagen's "humanness" at hitting a golf ball endeared him to galleries everywhere. Knowing there was no such thing as the perfect round, "The Haig" simply moved on to the task at hand — playing the next shot. Sir Walter recorded a still-unsurpassed PGA mark of 22 consecutive wins in match play during that remarkable stretch. In all, he would claim five PGA Championships.

4.

Jack Attack at Augusta

I'm not retiring now. I'm not that smart.

> *Jack Nicklaus,*
> *after winning the 50th Masters*
> *— his 20th major championship*
> *— at the age of 46*

The Golden Bear had become the Olden Bear by April 1986. Few gave the great Jack Nicklaus a devil's chance in heaven of winning a 20th major championship at Augusta National. But peeling back the years, the Bear once again finds the bite to make one last glorious run — at the grand old age of 46. Scorching the back nine for an eye-popping 30, Nicklaus records six birdies and an eagle on the last 10 holes. One final time Jack Nicklaus has played like, well, Jack Nicklaus.

3.

Hogan's Miraculous Comeback

Just 16 months after a near-fatal head-on colli-sion with a Greyhound bus leaves him with a double-fractured pelvis, a broken left ankle, a fractured collarbone and broken rib, Bantam Ben Hogan wins the 1950 U.S. Open, the second of his four U.S. Open titles. Courageously limping from hole to hole, the steel-willed Hogan has to play a grueling 36 holes on the final day of play at Merion Cricket Club just outside Philadelphia. Hogan manages a tie at the end of regular play, forcing a playoff the following day, which he wins by four strokes.

I feel like I'm a hundred years old.

Byron Nelson,
after winning the 1945 PGA Championship,
his ninth win in a row on his way
to 11 consecutive victories that year

2.

Nelson's Incredible 11 Straight PGA Tour Wins

In 1945, Byron Nelson makes history with the most amazing consecutive win streak in PGA annals — 11 straight.

Some skeptics claim his mark, made during the World War II years, is bereft of quality competition. But if Sam Snead and Ben Hogan aren't considered first-rate fare, who is?

Actually, during the first 10 events of '45, Snead holds a 6-4 victory advantage over Nelson. Then Lord Byron heats up. Included in the record run is the PGA Championship at Dayton. Nelson goes on to collect 18 wins for the year and register an unbelievable total of 320 below par for the season! It is considered to be the greatest golfing feat ever behind Bobby Jones' immortal Grand Slam in 1930.

1.

Golf's Immortal Mark — the Jones Grand Slam

With his game finely tuned even by his own standards, the redoubtable Bobby Jones embarks on the 1930 season with a singular mission in mind: to win golf's four major championships in the same year.

He opens by winning the one major he previously had failed to win in his peerless career — the British Amateur. Next comes the British Open, where Jones gets off to a flat start before regaining his touch and holding off two late chargers. Back in the States, The Emperor pulls out a strong 68 in the third round to push him ahead in the U.S. Open; three down — one to go.

And finally, at the Merion Cricket Club near Philadelphia, Jones outdistances his amateur rivals in a week of match play to claim the U.S. Amateur title — the last leg of the Grand Slam.

The Masters, which Jones helped found, and the PGA Championship have replaced the two amateur jewels in the modern Slam. Still, many feel Jones' achievement is the finest individual performance in the history of sports.

Chapter 5

The 20 Toughest Courses in the World

God builds golf courses. Men just go out and find them.
Robert Trent Jones

"Greatest" lists galore have been published on the subject of golf courses. Here we attempt to place the *toughest* tests for your consideration. Gathered from a medley of sources, including books, media guides, magazines, the players and even the architects, subjectivity rules the day: A mountainous challenge in terms of length might be chicken feed for a Daly, a Woods or a Nicklaus. On the other hand, a tight layout might be advantageous to a shotmaking wizard like Watson or Hogan, but might invite panic for an unbridled long hitter.

Esteemed modern-day golf architect Pete Dye was asked in the early 1980s to design the toughest course in the world. The PGA West (Stadium Course), in La Quinta, California, was his reply. Yet the vote is still out on where Dye's monster will ultimately be placed, if at all, in golf-architecture history.

If you feel you possess the heart of Hogan and the courage of Indiana Jones, proceed to the following pages. But be forewarned: This Top 20 "toughest" is not for the faint of heart. Band-Aids and CPR not administered.

20.
Baltusrol (Lower)
Springfield, NJ. Date of origin: 1922
Architect(s): A.W. Tillinghast

19.
Tournament Players Club at Sawgrass
(Stadium Course)
Ponte Vedra, FL (1980)
Pete Dye

18.
Princeville (Prince Course)
Kauai, Hawaii (1990)
Robert Trent Jones, Jr.

17.
Oakmont
Oakmont, PA (1903)
William and Henry Fownes

16.
Royal Dornoch
Dornoch, Scotland (1886)

The TPC at Sawgrass is *Star Wars* golf. The place was designed by Darth Vader.

Ben Crenshaw

I'm not very good at landing a 5-iron on the hood of a car.

Jack Nicklaus' critique of TPC at Sawgrass

Oakmont is a course where good putters worry about their second shot before they hit the first one.

Lew Worsham,
1947 U.S. Open champion

I'm glad I brought this course, this monster, to its knees.

Ben Hogan,
after his 1951 U.S. Open win at Oakland Hills

To match par on Winged Foot, you've got to be luckier than a dog with two tails.

Sam Snead

15.

PGA West (Stadium Course)
La Quinta, CA (1986)
Pete Dye

14.

Oakland Hills (South Course)
Birmingham, MI (1918)
Donald Ross, Robert Trent Jones

13.

Winged Foot (West Course)
Mamaroneck, NY (1923)
A.W. Tillinghast

12.

Carnoustie
Carnoustie, Scotland (circa 1500)

11.

Olympic (Lakeside Course)
San Francisco, CA (1924)
Wilfrid Reid, Sam Whiting

Carnoustie is the most masculine golf course in the world. It's got hair on its chest, and under the hair there's a tattoo.

David Boyd

The man who doesn't feel emotionally stirred when he golfs at Pinehurst, beneath those clear blue skies and with the pine fragrance in his nostrils, is one who should be ruled out of golf for life.

Tommy Armour

10.

Pinehurst No. 2

Pinehurst, NC (1925)
Donald Ross

9.

Royal Melbourne

Melbourne, Australia (1926)
Alister Mackenzie, Alex Russell

8.

Seminole

North Palm Beach, FL (1929)
Donald Ross

7.

Muirfield

Gullane, Scotland (1891)
Old Tom Morris

6.

Merion Cricket Club (East Course)

Ardmore, PA (1912)
Hugh Wilson

The Old Course is a phenomenon. The ultimate beauty of it is that it is not fair, and in that it approximates life. You can do all the planning you like, but in the end the Old Course has the final say.

Alec Beveridge,
secretary of St. Andrews

The Old Course has a tendency to bring out the best in a player's game, and the worst. She's not meant for ordinary golf.

Tom Watson,
retired Edinburgh car mechanic
who owns a cottage at St. Andrews

You've got to respect the old gal.

Greg Norman,
on Augusta National

Cypress Point is the Sistine Chapel of Golf

Frank Tatum
former USGA president

It's an examination in golf.

Bernard Darwin,
on Pine Valley

5.

St. Andrews (Old Course)
St. Andrews Fife, Scotland (circa 1770)*

4.

Augusta National
Augusta, GA (1932)
Alister Mackenzie, Bobby Jones, Jr.

3.

Cypress Point
Monterey Peninsula, CA (1928)
Alister Mackenzie

2.

Pine Valley
Clementon, NJ (1922)
George Crump, Harvey S. Colt

* Golf on the site of St. Andrews, Scotland was played as early as the 1400s. The Old Course itself, however, was not laid out until the mid-1760s.

This place isn't the Louvre. It's everything that's *in* the Louvre too, with all the artists gathered around.

Bing Crosby,
on Pebble Beach Golf Links

Alcatraz with grass.

Bob Hope,
on Pebble Beach

1.

Pebble Beach Golf Links

Monterey Peninsula, CA (1919)
Jack Neville, Douglas Grant

Chapter 6

NINE HOLES
FROM HADES

It is ironic that some of the places on a golf course that look the most like heaven are, in truth, the most devilish places to play. Listed on the following pages are nine holes that have historically provided fits for even golf's finest. Naturally, there are thousands more like them around the world, but these Infamous Nine will not only play you tough, they may even bring you to your knees — in prayer.

9.

The 5th at Pine Valley

Clementon, NJ — par 3, 221 yards

Deep ravine from tee to green. Sand guards the left side of a long narrow green that slopes to the right. A quagmire of pine roots to the green's right offers a complex and severe hazard.

8.

The 15th at Oakmont

Oakmont, PA — par 4, 453 yards

The toughest hole on one of the toughest courses in the world. Johnny Miller birdied it when he fired his final-round 63, a U.S. Open record, in winning the 1973 Open.

7.

The 17th at Carnoustie

Carnoustie, Scotland — par 4, 454 yards

One of the famous three finishing holes at Carnoustie, the 17th demands an accurately placed drive on a peninsular pocket of land formed by the Barry Burn (stream), which winds back and forth across the fairway.

6.
The 3rd at Starr Pass
Tucson, AZ — par 4, 430 yards

The toughest hole, scoring-wise, on the PGA Tour in 1996. You tee off into prevailing winds onto a slim driving area, with snug out of bounds left and right. A sheer, natural rock-wall face, 18-feet high, lies 30 yards out from an elevated green.

5.
The 8th at Royal Troon
Troon, Scotland — par 3, 126 yards

The world-renowned "Postage Stamp" hole is an elevated green approximately a dozen feet above a series of deep bunkers surrounding it. Viewers got a look at how the miniscule hole can manhandle a superstar, when Tiger Woods took an inglorious triple-bogey on it in the 1997 British Open, killing any hopes he had for making a run at the title.

4.

The 8th at Pebble Beach

Monterey Peninsula, CA — par 4, 431yards

Picking the toughest hole on the world's toughest course is...well, tough. Eight of the course's 18 holes are ocean holes. On the 8th, your drive is up a sloping incline that leaves little clue to the second shot. Cresting the slope, the fairway ends! Before you is a 100-foot drop off a sheer cliff. The green? 180 yards away over Carmel Bay. Happy golfing, friend.

3.

The 14th at St. Andrews

St. Andrews Fife, Scotland — par 5, 560 yards

Known as "The Long," this challenging par five on the Old Course actually is considered more testing than its famous companion three holes hence — the 17th "Road Hole." As far back as 1901, an opinion poll written up in an English periodical entitled *Golf Illustrated* rated The Long as one of the two best long holes in the British Isles. At that time, that meant the world.

2.

The 12th at Augusta National
Augusta, GA — par 3, 155 yards

The hub of the famous Amen Corner, the "Golden Bell" as the 12th is known, extends only the slightest margin for error. A critical pitch across Rae's Creek to a sliver of green with one front and two rear bunkers awaits the bold shotmaker. Swirling winds in this low section of Augusta National add a macabre dimension to the tee shot, making club selection vital. Even veteran pros usually play it safe, aiming for the larger left side of the green.

1.

The 16th at Cypress Point
Monterey Peninsula, CA — par 3, 233 yards

Considered by many to be the most spectacular hole in golf, this gem of a par 3 has a truly unique physical property about it — a completely blue fairway. As in the Pacific Ocean. Tee to green, nothing but ocean. Make that 233 yards worth. Better fill your golf bag with a fresh supply of balls.

Chapter 7

WOMEN'S GOLF: THE ELITE EIGHT

8.

Louise Suggs

After a successful amateur career that included victories in both the U.S. and British Women's Amateur, Suggs turned pro in 1948. Before she placed her clubs in her bag for the final time, the smooth swinger from Atlanta had racked up 50 LPGA Tour victories, including 11 majors. She is a founding member of the LPGA and one of the original inductees into the LPGA Hall of Fame in 1951.

7.

Patty Berg

Considered the first ambassador of women's golf, Berg still holds the LPGA record for most victories in major tournaments with 15. She is a founder and charter member of the LPGA and also served as its first president. Berg still sits third on the all-time wins list, with 57 professional victories, and is a three-time Vare Trophy winner (lowest scoring average). She had an outstanding amateur career, which included 29 wins, before turning pro. No woman is said to have contributed more to women's golf than Berg.

6.

Nancy Lopez

As a young pro in just her second season on the LPGA Tour, Lopez became a phenomenon. She took nine tour titles that year, including her first of three majors. But what created a media stir was her blistering streak of five consecutive victories, an LPGA modern record. She was named Player of the Year, and women's golf attendance soared like never before. The LPGA had a new superstar and Lopez's affable personality helped make her one of the sports world's most popular figures. In her career, Lopez has compiled 47 tour victories and has been named Player of the Year four times.

5.

Glenna Collett

She was called "The Female Bobby Jones" and held claim to being the top woman golfer in America during the 1920s. Collett rode her prodigious driving ability (she once launched a tee shot 307 yards) to the heights of women's golf, once winning, in 1924, 59 of 60 matches. Her two celebrated duels with Britain's Joyce Wethered both ended in defeat, but there was little else to diminish her brilliant record. Over a glowing 14-year period, Collett collected six national championship crowns.

4.

Kathy Whitworth

The LPGA's all-time career leader in victories with 88, Whitworth dominated women's play from the mid-1960s through the middle of the following decade. Along the way, she staged some great matches with rivals Mickey Wright and Carol Mann. Whitworth claimed six major championships in her career, but not unlike her male counterpart, Sam Snead — the PGA Tour's all-time career wins leader who never won the U.S. Open — she could never find the handle on the U.S. Women's Open trophy. It would be the only major championship she would fail to win.

3.

Mickey Wright

Shy, unassuming Mickey Wright led the women's tour for seven years in the late 1950s through the mid-'60s. During her reign, Wright recorded a whopping 82 LPGA tour victories, including four LPGA championships, four U.S. Opens and five Vare Trophies. The development and finesse of her swing technique invoked comparisons to both Ben Hogan and Bobby Jones. In all, she garnered 13 major titles on her way to the LPGA Hall of Fame.

2.

Babe Didrikson Zaharias

Still considered to be the greatest woman athlete of all time, Babe reigned for a period of 20 years in women's golf and was a charter member of the LPGA Tour. She won more than 50 amateur and professional titles, including three U.S. Opens, and became the first American to win the British Ladies' Open Amateur Championship, in 1947. Before taking up golf at the suggestion of sportswriter Grantland Rice, in 1933, she had won two gold medals in the 1932 Olympic Games in track and field.

But her crowning accomplishment came in her battle against cancer, courageously competing and winning seven more tournaments after cancer surgery in 1953, including her third U.S. Open. She died in 1956, at the age of 42.

I have never played golf with anyone, man or woman, amateur or professional, who made me feel so utterly outclassed. I have no hesitancy in saying she is the finest golfer I have ever seen.

Bobby Jones, Jr.
on Joyce Wethered

Miss Wethered brought power combined with a perfection of style and a hitherto unknown degree of accuracy into women's golf.

Enid Wilson,
three-time Ladies' British Amateur champion

She had the most correct and loveliest swing golf had ever known. If you were an American woman golfer, you could thank your lucky stars that there was only one Joyce Wethered and that she lived in England.

Herbert Warren Wind

1.

Joyce Wethered

She has been called by many the finest golfer who ever lived, and *not* just in the women's ranks. Wethered dominated British golf in the 1920s. Her brilliant career, not unlike that of Bobby Jones, was relatively short — mainly because there were no new worlds to conquer. Wethered won the English Ladies' Amateur five straight times and the Ladies' British Open Amateur on four occasions. Her greatest match, at least the one generating the most publicity, came in 1929. Coming out of a four-year retirement, Wethered, for the second time in her career, met America's great champion Glenna Collett. They squared off head on at St. Andrews in the Ladies' British Open Amateur finals. But Collett, 5-up at one point, could not contain her opponent's charge, and Wethered (later Lady Heathcoat-Amory) notched her ninth and last major championship.

Top Five Defining Moments for Women's Golf

5.

United States wins Women's World Amateur Team Championship in 1970, in Madrid, when France's superb Catherine Lacoste unaccountably collapses during the final nine, dropping four strokes to the USA's Martha Wilkinson, who nails down a one-stroke American victory.

4.

Kathy Whitworth's all-time leading 88 LPGA Tour victories, the most career wins by any professional golfer ever.

3.

Britian's **Joyce Wethered** defeats top American golfer Glenna Collett in the first of their two match-play meetings, in 1925 at Royal Troon, during the Ladies' British Open Amateur. Four years later, Wethered comes out of retirement to again beat Collett in the same tournament — a sensational match that is hailed as the unofficial championship of the world at the time.

2.

Nancy Lopez's LPGA-record five-consecutive tour victories in 1978, including the first of her three LPGA Championships.

1.

Babe Didrikson Zaharias' courageous comeback from cancer surgery to win the 1954 U.S. Women's Open.

Dynamic Double

In 1924, a sporting feat of rarefied proportions is executed by an exceptional woman athlete — Mary K. Browne. Two weeks prior to the women's national golf championship, Browne reaches the semifinals of the U.S. Women's Tennis Championship at Forest Hills, taking the renowned Helen Wills to three sets before losing. Switching to the links for the U.S. Women's Championship, Browne goes on a tear, upsetting the reigning queen of American golf, Glenna Collett, in the semifinals. Though she loses in the finals, Browne's display of versatility places her on a par with the great Babe Didrikson Zaharias for pure athletic achievement.

We suggest that the limit of a lady's drive can be no longer than 70 to 80 yards, not because we doubt a lady's power to make a longer drive, but because that cannot well be done without raising the club above the shoulder. Now we do not presume to dictate, but we must observe that the posture and gestures requisite for a full swing are not particularly graceful when the player is clad in female dress.

Lord Wellwood, 1890

Chapter 8

MOSTS, BESTS & FIRSTS

America's First Nine-Hole Course:

Brenton's Point, near Newport, RI, in 1890.

The First Manicured Course in the United States, Complete with Clubhouse:

Shinnecock Hills, on Long Island, in 1891. Designed by Scotland's Willie Dunn.

Most Shots Under Par, 72 Holes:

28 — John Huston, 1998 Hawaiian Open

27 — Ben Hogan, 1945 Portland Invitational
　　　Mike Souchak, 1955 Texas Open

Lowest All-time PGA Tour Score, 72 holes:

257 — Mike Souchak, 1955 Texas Open

Lowest All-Time PGA Score, 18 Holes:

59 — Al Geiberger, 1977 Memphis Classic
　　　Chip Beck, 1991 Las Vegas Invitational

Most Birdies in a Row:

8 — Bob Goalby, 1961 St. Petersburg Open
Fuzzy Zoeller, 1976 Quad Cities Open
Dewey Arnette, 1987 Buick Open

Most PGA Victories, Career:

81 — Sam Snead
70 — Jack Nicklaus

Most Consecutive Years Winning at Least One PGA Tour Event:

17 — Arnold Palmer, Jack Nicklaus

Most Consecutive PGA Tour Victories:

11 — Byron Nelson in 1945

6 — Ben Hogan in 1948

Most Victories in a Single Event:

8 — Sam Snead, Greater Greensboro Open

6 — Alex Ross, North & South Open
    Sam Snead, Miami Open
    Jack Nicklaus, Masters

Most Consecutive Victories in a Single Event:

4 — Walter Hagen, PGA Championship: 1924-1927;
    Gene Sarazen, Miami Open: 1926, (none in '27)
    1928-1930

Most Victories in a Calendar Year:

18 — Byron Nelson, 1945
13 — Ben Hogan, 1946
11 — Sam Snead, 1950

Most Consecutive Events without Missing the Cut:

113 — Byron Nelson, during mid-1940s
105 — Jack Nicklaus, Nov. 1970 – September 1976

Oldest Winners:

Sam Snead — 52 years 10 months, 8 days
(1965 Greater Greensboro Open)
Art Wall — 51 years, 7 months 10 days
(1975 Greater Milwaukee Open)

Most Number of Decades Winning at Least One PGA Tour Event:

4 — Sam Snead, Ray Floyd

Most Holes-in-One, Career (Men):

Art Wall, longtime PGA touring pro, with 40. Most recently in 1973, on the 196-yard 16th hole at Inverrary, Lauderhill, FL. Thirty-eight of his aces were recorded at Pocono Manor in the Pocono Mountains, Pennsylvania.

Most Holes in One, LPGA Tour, Career:

Kathy Whitworth, 11

Longest Hole-in-One:

444 yards — Robert Mitera, Omaha, NE, on the 10th hole at Miracle Hills Golf Course, October 7, 1965

Longest Drivers

Honorable Mention:

Chick Harbert, 1940s (won over 40 long-driving contests in 13 years on PGA tour)

10. **Fuzzy Zoeller**
 9. **Mike Souchak**
 8. **Greg Norman**
 7. **Sam Snead**
 6. **Jimmy Thomson** (Scotland 1920s, '30s and '40s)
 5. **Jack Nicklaus**
 4. **Jim Dent**
 3. **John Daly**
 2. **George Bayer** (won 12 of 13 driving contests as tour rookie in 1955. Once drove the 426-yard 7th hole at El Rio during the Tucson Open in the 1950s)
 1. **Tiger Woods**

The Ole Don Johnson "Tin Cup" Sucker Drive

From the north end of Lake Agawam, "Uncle Samuel" Parrish of Shinnecock Hills, Southhampton, NY, drove a shot over an iced lake that, when it hit the ice, continued with "little diminution" till it came to rest on the opposite shore, 489$^{1}/_{2}$ yards away (self-paced by Parrish), in the late 1880s.

For a short time, with no particulars having been given, Samuel enjoyed the reputation of a long driver and was the recipient of "very many hearty congratulations."

Best Long Iron Hitters

10. **Seve Ballesteros**
9. **Byron Nelson**
8. **Ben Hogan**
7. **Arnold Palmer**
6. **Sam Snead**
5. **Hale Irwin**
4. **Tiger Woods**
3. **Tommy Armour**
2. **Bobby Jones, Jr.**
1. **Jack Nicklaus**

Best Medium Iron Players

5. **Bobby Locke**
4. **Johnny Miller**
3. **Cary Middlecoff**
2. **Walter Hagen**
1. **Bobby Jones**

Wizards with the Wedge

Honorable Mention:
Sam Snead
Gene Sarazen
Craig Stadler
Ray Floyd

10. **Johnny Miller**
 9. **Tom Watson**
 8. **Johnny Revolta**
 7. **Chi Chi Rodriguez**
 6. **Lee Trevino**
 5. **Walter Hagen**
 4. **Corey Pavin**
 3. **Norman Von Nida**
 2. **Julius Boros**
 1. **Gary Player**

Greatest All-Time Putters

Honorable Mention:

Paul Azinger

Jerry Barber

Bob Charles

Horton Smith

Willie Park, Jr. (British Open winner 1887, 1889. Said to have practiced putting six hours a day. Reputed to be "deadliest putter golf had ever seen.")

10. **Walter Hagen**
 9. **Dave Stockton**
 8. **Billy Casper**
 7. **Tom Watson**
 6. **Jack Nicklaus**
 5. **Arnold Palmer**
 4. **Walter J. Travis**
 3. **George Archer**
 2. **Bobby Locke**
 1. **Ben Crenshaw**

Gene Littler swings a golf club with the same elegant style Sinatra brings to a song, Nureyev to a dance, Olivier to a Shakespearean role. If his swing were a piece of music, it would be a Strauss waltz.

Nick Seitz

If you want to copy one swing, copy his.

Johnny Miller,
on Al Geiberger

Swingin' Sam Meets Slingin' Sam

If golf were pro football, he'd be Sammy Baugh. Same first names, one-syllable last names — both bringing consummate grace and art to their work. If golf and football were diving competitions, they would earn 5.9s for artistic merit. Forget that he's the all-time No. 1 career leader in wins, Sam Snead has the prettiest swing you ever saw.

All-Time Sweetest Swings

10. **Payne Stewart**
 9. **Johnny Miller**
 8. **Al Geiberger**
 7. **Tom Weiskopf**
 6. **Bruce Crampton**
 5. **Harry Vardon**
 4. **Bobby Jones, Jr.**
 3. **Tiger Woods**
 2. **Gene Littler**
 1. **Sam Snead**

Best Pressure Shots

(listed chronologically)

1922 — **Walter Hagen**, British Open; final round, 15th hole

1923 — **Bobby Jones**, U.S. Open; playoff, 18th hole

1935 — **Gene Sarazen**, Masters; final round, 15th hole

1939 — **Byron Nelson**, U.S. Open; second playoff round, 4th hole

1951 — **Byron Nelson**, Crosby at Cypress Point; second round, 17th hole

1972 — **Lee Trevino**, British Open; third-round, 16th, 17th holes

1972 — **Gary Player**, 1972 PGA; final round, 16th hole

1976 — **Jerry Pate**, 1976 U.S. Open; final round, 18th hole

1982 — **Tom Watson**, U.S. Open; final round, 17th hole

1986 — **Bob Tway**, PGA Championship; final round, 18th hole

1987 — **Larry Mize**, Masters; second playoff hole (11th)

Best Golf Club Thrower:

Tommy Bolt

Chapter 9

MIXED BAG

English Eloquence

A curious sport whose object is to put a very small ball in a very small hole with implements ill-designed for the purpose.

Sir Winston Churchill,
on golf

Golf is an open exhibition of overweening ambition, courage deflated by stupidity, skill soured by a whiff of arrogance. These humiliations are the essence of the game.

Alistair Cooke

Golf was just what the Scottish character had been seeking for centuries, namely, a method of self-torture.

Alistair Cooke

Presidential Players

"Stick out your fanny, Mr. President."
> *Sam Snead's advice*
> *to President Dwight D. Eisenhower*

Teddy Roosevelt found golf too mild a sport for his liking, but the golfing bug went on to bite many an American chief executive. Among those who have thrashed their way around the fairways:

> William McKinley
> Warren G. Harding
> William Howard Taft
> Woodrow Wilson
> Dwight D. Eisenhower
> Gerald Ford
> George Bush
> Bill Clinton

Favorite Henry Longhurst Story

Famed British golf writer Henry Longhurst tells a memorable story of his longtime pal from the ranks of the distinguished: Valentine Viscount Castlerosse, the 6th Earl of Kenmare, and "every inch a Lord." Castlerosse, having a particularly bad round of golf one day with his friend Longhurst at Walton Heath, uttered these epic words to his caddie on the final hole, "Pick it up, have the clubs destroyed, and leave the course at once."

Hard Stuff

The hardest shot is the mashie at 90 yards from the green, where the ball has to be played against an oak tree, bounces back into a sandtrap, hits a stone, bounces on the green and then rolls into the cup. That shot is so difficult I have made it only once.

Zeppo Marx

I am undecided as to which of these two is the hardest shot in golf for me — any unconceded putt or the explosion shot off the first tee. Both have caused me more strokes than I care to write about.

Ring Lardner

I am stumped when it comes to saying which is the hardest shot in golf for me, but I know the easiest one — the first shot at the 19th hole.

W.C. Fields

I find the hardest shot in golf is a hole-in-one.

Groucho Marx

The Vrootengrud Legend — The *Real* Happy Gilmore

In 1900, a 61-year-old aborigine caddy named Vrootengrud made consecutive holes-in-one on the same hole — the tough par-3 17th at Melbourne's Imperial Golf Club — while caddying in a match between two leading professionals. When the man he was caddying for failed twice to drive the green, courageously attempting to drive a 1200-foot deep canyon that fronted the green, Vrootengrud asked for the opportunity to try it himself. Using what appeared to be a club looking more like a walking stick, Vrootengrud addressed the ball from 10 feet behind. Running up to it, à la Adam Sandler in the movie *Happy Gilmore,* Vrootengrud laced consecutive shots into the cup 265 yards away, clearing the canyon both times.

It is considered by many to be the greatest feat in golf history. The event was witnessed by "a record crowd" who had assembled to see the two professional champions play.

Scariest Moment in Golf History

Lee Trevino, Jerry Heard and Bobby Nichols are struck by lightning on the 13th hole of the Western Open at the Butler National Golf Club outside Chicago, on June 27, 1975. Quipped Trevino the following day from the hospital intensive care unit, "They'll probably slap a two-stroke penalty on me for slow play."

Serenity, Calamity, Reptility

Serenity is knowing your worst shot is still going to be pretty good.

Johnny Miller

"Calamity Jane" — the name of Bobby Jones' putter.

Playing with a hook is like playing with a pocketful of rattlesnakes.

Ben Hogan

Listen to the Wind

There is no other loser in sports as gracious and warm as Jack Nicklaus has shown himself to be.

Herbert Warren Wind

The post-war rivalry between Ben Hogan and Byron Nelson did not prove who was the better golfer. It would be unfair to either to say that the other had demonstrated even a slight superiority. When Hogan did something remarkable, Nelson invariably came up with a matching performance, and vice versa.

Herbert Warren Wind

Links

Linksland is the stretch of sandy soil deposited by the sea as it receded slowly over the centuries. The soil drains well and produces splendid turf for golf.

Herbert Warren Wind

I know of one course in the United States that is close to being a true links course, and that is Sankaty Head, on the island of Nantucket, off the southeast coast of Massachusetts. Sankaty Head is not immediately on the sea, but it is duney and sandy-soiled, windswept, treeless, and natural — a wonderful course. By no coincidence, it was designed by Donald Ross, Dornoch's most famous native son, who, as an architect, endeavored to create a linksland element in every course he built (Pinehurst No. 2, Oakland Hills, Inverness, Oak Hill, among others).

Michael Bamburger

The "Open" Market

Actress Fay Wray introduced Walter Hagen to the crowd gathered at the first tee of the 1929 PGA Championship in Los Angeles as "the Opium Champion of Great Britain."

Golf is an indispensable adjunct of high civilization.
Andrew Carnegie

INDEX

Index

156

About the Author

Sports historian and writer Alan Ross lives with his wife in Monteagle, Tennessee. A graduate of Fordham University, he is a former editor for Professional Team Publications, Athlon Sports Communications, and Walnut Grove Press. His feature articles on sports history have appeared in *The Sporting News*, *Lindy's*, *Athlon Sports*, *Athletic Administration*, *Game Day*, *NFL Insider*, *Arizona Cardinals Media Guide*, and *Track Record*. In the mid-1970s, Ross wrote a weekly poem recapping the previous week's sports news for *The Tennessean*. He has authored two other books, *Hooked on Hockey* and *Echoes from the Ball Park*.